THE BLESSINGS OF
DISAPPOINTMENT

THE BLESSINGS OF
DISAPPOINTMENT

JOHN D. CADORE

Other Books by this Author

Seven Years of Tribulation

The Road to Recovery

The Habits of Consistency Perseverance &
Appreciation

ISBN: 979-8-8693-4046-7 Paperback
ISBN: 979-8-8693-4048-1 Hardback
ISBN: 979-8-8693-4047-4 eBook

Book Orders:

Law Office of John D. Cadore
34 Chenango Street
Binghamton, NY 13901
Phone: 607-777-9407
Or may be ordered through booksellers online.

This book is printed on acid-free paper.

DEDICATION

This book is dedicated to my two sons, Austin and Joshua.

I am very proud of the men you are becoming.

I am equally proud of both of your successes at this stage in your young lives.

This book should serve as a reminder that there is no such thing as failure.

Contents

CHAPTER ONE

THE LIFE OF JOSEPH

When writing about the blessings of disappointments, the best and one of the most deserving stories to begin with is the life of Joseph as told in the Book of Genesis.

THE STORY OF JOSEPH: FROM PRISON TO PRINCE

Joseph was one of the twelve tribes of Israel, a son of Jacob and his wife Rachel. Known as "the righteous one," he was favored by his father who gave him a special-colored coat, and sold by his brothers to Egypt, where he ultimately became ruler of the land, second only to King Pharaoh.

One day, Jacob instructed Joseph to visit his brothers in Shechem, where they were tending their sheep. Little did he know that this would be the last time he would see his dear son, until their reunion a long twenty-two years later. (Chabad. org)

Seizing their chance, the brothers threw the unsuspecting Joseph into a pit. A short while later they spotted an Arab caravan passing the scene, and the brothers sold Joseph to the traders. Joseph was eventually brought to Egypt, where he was sold to Potiphar, one of King Pharaoh's ministers (Chabad.org)

For a while, things started to look up for young Joseph. Divine success enabled him to find favor in his master's eyes, and he was appointed head of Potiphar's estate. However, this did not last long.

Attracted by Joseph's handsome looks, Potiphar's wife desired to be intimate with him. To her consternation, Joseph continuously refused. One day when they were both alone, Potiphar's wife grabbed Joseph's garment, and demanded that he consent. Thinking quickly, Joseph slid out of his cloak and ran outside. The self-control earned the appellation "Joseph the righteous." (Chabad.org)

But Potiphar's wife turned the tables on Joseph, telling her husband that it was Joseph who had tried to entice her. Potiphar reacted by placing his trustworthy assistant in prison.

JOSEPH, THE DREAM INTERPRETER

When the King's royal cupbearer and baker were imprisoned, Joseph successfully interpreted their dreams, correctly predicting that the cupbearer would be released, and the baker hanged.

Two years later, King Pharaoh himself envisioned two dreams which none of his advisors were able to explain. Remembering the Hebrew youth from his prison days, the cupbearer suggested that Joseph be summoned. Joseph, then thirty, interpreted Pharaoh's dreams being a divine prediction for seven years of plenty, followed by seven years of famine, and advised Pharaoh to prepare by storing grain during the first seven years. Impressed by Joseph's wisdom,

Pharaoh appointed him as viceroy, second only to the King himself, and tasked him with readying the nation for the years of famine. (Chabad.org)

EFFECTS OF THE FAMINE AND JOSEPH'S FAMILY REUNION

The effect of the famine was felt in nearby Canaan. Hearing that there was grain in Egypt, Joseph's brothers journeyed there to buy precious food from the viceroy, not realizing that he was their own brother.

Joseph decided to utilize this opportunity to observe whether his brothers truly regretted having sold him. Joseph tested his brothers' determination to save their youngest brother Benjamin, Joseph's only natural brother. Joseph then revealed his identity to his astonished siblings. (Chabad.org)

Following their family reunion, Jacob and his family eventually settled in the Goshen section of Egypt. This series of events served as the backdrop for Israel's ultimate enslavement in Egypt and subsequent exodus. (Chabad.org)

The story of Joseph is believed by many to be the hidden story of the life of Jesus.

THE BLESSINGS OF RESTORATION

In many Christian circles, I have heard The Blessings of Restoration referred to as the Miracle of Restoration. Both the blessing of restoration and the miracle of restoration can be observed in the life of Joseph and the life of Job. Both biblical men restored with at least double what they have lost. In the case of Job, he was restored double his livestock, wealth and children, and Joseph became the Prime Minister of Egypt under the rule of the Pharaoh. In that position Joseph was able to prepare the nation of Egypt for an impending famine, and in so doing, was able to feed his hungry long-lost family.

When studying the life of Joseph, we can learn that there are usually unknown and unthinkable reasons why people face disappointment. As Joseph himself said to his brothers, "What you meant for evil, the Lord meant it for good." Joseph's purpose was primarily to be caretakers of people during the periods when they were unable to take care of themselves. It is widely believed, that had it not been for Joseph being the prime minister of Egypt during the times of famine, they would have been much more widespread starvation throughout the land of Egypt. Also of major significance is that he would not have been able to care for his aging father, Jesse, and his untrustworthy brothers.

Throughout the life of Joseph, one can see the hand of Satan and the hand of God. Always, without any exception, the hand of God would prevail over the wicked hands of Satan.

Another way one may want to look at this story, or another conclusion that may be drawn from both the lives of Joseph and Job, is that Satan is a loser and he would always be a loser. Any success made by Satan is usually short-lived and would always be made subservient to the will and desires of God.

One can conclude that in the case of Satan "once a loser, always a loser." His worldly and carnal pleasure on this earth would be short-lived, and eventually he would be in his rightful place, the Bottomless Pit.

CHAPTER TWO

THE LIFE OF JOB

In the well-known biblical story dealing with the problems of undeserved suffering, Job loses his children, his possessions, and his health. Job's wife, after observing his struggles said to her husband, "Do you still persist in your integrity?" Curse God and die. (Job 2:9)

She cannot bear her husband's blind acceptance of the tragedies that befall them. (Job 19:17)

Job's initial response to his wife's provocative suggestion is harsh. "You speak as any woman would speak. Shall we receive the good at the hand of God and not receive the bad?" (Job 2:10)

Job's wife is conspicuously absent from the happy ending in which Job's world is restored. Job's dead children spring back to life, as it were, because he ends up having, as in the beginning, seven sons and three daughters.

One important lesson to take away from the life of Job is that in the end he was restored with twice as much as he owned before his troubles with Satan began.

The story of Job reinforces an age-old saying that behind every dark cloud, there is a silver lining. However, the silver lining would only be seen after the dark cloud has receded. This is also a story of perseverance. Whether in worldly or biblical terms, treasures usually await those that will persevere.

Life is a journey. It can also be a marathon. It is not a sprint. The length of a marathon is 26.2 miles. Not everyone is gifted with the stamina, the will and determination to run a marathon.

There is a saying that "one will either grow old or die young." I believe that what really matters is growing old and acquiring wisdom. The Bible states, without vision, the people will perish, (Proverbs 29:18)

Where there is no vision, the people perish. Without a vision, people are doomed to wander aimlessly. In this context, vision and wisdom can be used interchangeably.

The life of Job gives real meaning to the slogan "forward ever, backward never." Job, throughout his nine months of tribulation, never gave up or stopped believing in God. In fact, when Job's wife suggested that he curse God and die, Job called her a fool. Instead of cursing God as his wife suggested, he said, "The Lord giveth and the Lord taketh away."

Job was totally correct in his assessment of many things, but he was partially incorrect in this statement. It was not the Lord that was his taking his earthly belongings away, it was the work of Satan that was attempting to make a convert of Job. This chapter provides a perfect example of the saying the delay and disappointments does not mean denial, failure or defeat.

CHAPTER THREE

THE KEY TO RECOVERY FROM SETBACKS

The basic key to surviving or recovering from any disappointment is to never remain stagnant. One should always keep moving and keep putting one foot in front of the other. Remaining constant or remaining at a standstill is one way to assure self- defeat.

To use a military analogy, it is very advantageous for any battalion in active combat to set as its goal to simply hold or maintain seized or conquered territory. An army in combat should have one major objective, which is the taking of additional territory. Whenever any army finds itself in a position where its goal is simply to maintain conquered territory, then the proper military strategy in many instances is to seek a treaty whereby the seized or conquered territory could be maintained. Just holding ground in the majority of life experiences is almost never enough.

Remaining constant or being satisfied with past victories is usually never good enough. Standing still, in and of itself, is the equivalent of setting oneself up for defeat. The first key in realizing blessings from disappointments is to never remain constant, or at a standstill. This is self-destructive and may very seldomly lead to recovery from the underlying disappointment.

Winners never quit and quitters never win. One should always remember that the bigger the disappointment, the greater the opportunity for self- fulfillment. The greater the opportunity, the greater would be the discouragement.

There is a reason that five percent of the people in the world lead the other ninety five percent of the world's population. Easily put, maybe the ninety five percent may have become too complacent with life's daily activities, and in many instances have resigned themselves to accept as fate and whatever obstacle that may find itself in their paths. To those people, my advice would be to be mindful that the greater the obstacle, the greater the opportunity for success.

One may not win every fight, nor would an army win every battle, but remember that it is much better to fail than to never try. I may go as far as even promising that in the not too long run, one's mess would eventually become their message. There would be no crown if one did not overcome the cross. The key message here is that during periods of obstacles and trial, one should never stand still. Standing still is one aspect of self-defeat.

CHAPTER FOUR

OUT OF EVIL COMETH GOOD: OVERCOMING

The key ingredient necessary for overcoming most unfavorable situations is perseverance. By perseverance, I am referring to not quitting. Quitters never win and winners never quit. Human beings can be overcomers both spiritually and carnally.

By spiritually I am referring to the basic knowledge that God is the Way, the Truth and the Light and that no problem or adversity is too large for him to overcome.

By overcoming carnally, I am referring to recognizing that, except in very few and isolated instances, success is reserved for individuals who possess the audacity and tenacity to persevere. One famous athlete, Mohammed Ali, once said that "will would always triumph over skill." Although it is very rewarding to be born with a high intelligence quotient, IQ, having been endowed with a high IQ is not, in and of itself, enough to guarantee success. Furthermore, in a vast majority of cases, average people with average IQs usually are more successful than individuals with very high IQs.

To be successful in any endeavor, one must have both the will and the skill to accomplish it. Having the skill in the endeavor may lead to a more successful outcome. It is also my belief that someone with a very strong will to accomplish a goal or a profession, while having average IQ for the profession or endeavor would attain greater satisfaction upon the completion of that project.

I am certain that over the years we have all known people with great IQs that failed to accomplish their goals. One might be tempted to say that certain obstacles encountered by those individuals prevented them from achieving their goal. The truth is that obstacles and setbacks are part of our daily lives. One must be able to persevere despite obstacles.

Within the arena of physical exercising and weightlifting, there is an adage that there is no gain without pain. This philosophy does not only apply to athletes and the activity of weightlifting, it is also applicable to everyday life. Once again, we should all remember that the bigger the challenge, the greater will be the prize. There is an old biblical saying, "through the fire, through the flood, before you get to your wealthy place." The wealthy place is analogous to the state of equilibrium. A state of equilibrium is described in physics, mathematics, and economics as a state of rest.

Within that arena, Emotional Quotient (EQ) should also be recognized as an important factor in success or failure. EQ measures one's responses to the ups and downs of the challenges faced in their daily life. Today, there are many scientists that have said that EQ, rather than IQ, is a better factor for predicting individual long run and short run successes. By long run, I am referring to periods of ten years and above; and by short run I am referring to periods of between two to ten years.

Whatever the time frame may be, an individual's drive to achieve success and his or her desire to persevere are two of the most important factors necessary for success. The road to success has always been under construction and it would continue to be under construction for generations to come.

CHAPTER FIVE

THE TRUTH ABOUT DIFFICULT AND HARD TIMES

It is my belief that the most productive periods in one's lifetime are usually brought about by tough, hard, or difficult times. The oxymoron about difficult times is that it is usually the most productive times in one's lifetime. It is the period or time when new ideas are realized, new plans are made from which the most worldly and unworldly progress is made. By unworldly, I am referring to faith-based achievements that are usually beneficial in the world to come.

Experience has led me to believe that a life without difficulties, and to some extent, tribulations, is a life not well lived. However, I am not in any way suggesting that one should engage in destructive behaviors that would certainly lead to troubles and in most instances, trouble with the legal system. Here, I am saying that even when one's intention is to be productive and law abiding, there exists the forces of evil whose intent would be destruction and chaos.

I do not believe it's possible for one to lead a productive and distinctive life without having a single enemy, or encounter people whose intent is to create roadblocks to progress. Roadblocks and impediments to progress also serve a beneficial purpose. They frequently cause one to look deep inside for solutions, possibilities, and opportunities that would otherwise have been ignored.

It is believed that individuals should not look for an easy life. But an easy and problem-free life is frequently a life without much meaning, with very little contribution to the growth, progress and productivity of society. We should ask, what if the civil rights leader Rosa Parks did not have the courage to not give up her seat on a bus to a white man. Where would America be today, had it not been for the struggles and contributions made by people like Martin Luther King, Jr.? Would America be a better place today were there no Medgar Evers and Elijah Cummings?

Although some people may answer the above two questions in the affirmative, it is my belief that most people would say that America and the world are a better place today because of them and many other people like them.

The question now to be asked is in what way individuals do and can improve their collective or individual lives because of hardship or tough times.

One note of importance is that people who experience tough or hard times and have prospered despite it, are usually not afraid to venture out in whatever arena they so desire, are more willing to take chances. Tough or difficult situations and experiences would usually make one better or bitter. Tough or difficult times would either lead to self- growth or it can act to stunt one's growth and progress.

I am of the belief that for most people currently residing on this planet, difficult times and tough situations would serve to expand their visions and horizons. In many instances, it can lead people to follow new avenues that they might have never thought of. Tough times never last; tough people do. This saying has proven to be true in the vast majority of situations faced by mankind.

It is widely believed by many that failure is the back door to success, and many people may attest that they owe their huge, moderate or average success to incidents in their lives, that were perceived by themselves and others as failure.

CHAPTER SIX

THE SIMILARITIES BEWEEN FAILURE AND DISAPPOINTMENT

Disappointment and failure are very similar in many respects. Both failure and disappointment are the back doors to success. One striking similarity between failure and disappointment is that they are excellent tools for learning. Many scholars said that the average individual will learn more from losing than he or she would from winning. Additionally, both failure and disappointment are great tools to build one's character. Within that same vein of thinking, it is important to remember that a quitter never wins, and a winner never quits.

Conventional wisdom has repeatedly taught us that the bigger and more difficult the challenge, the greater will be the prize.

This concept could be a bone of contention between a capitalist society versus a socialist or Marxist society. Basic knowledge has taught us that in socialist or Marxist societies, the government would usually provide a flow of services, education or job skills which the average member of the society would most likely never go below. However, usually when there exists a floor which no member of society would fall below, the flip side of such society is that there is usually a ceiling which no ordinary member of society can rise above.

Only the elite in such societies, usually the president and his close circle, friends, family and associates can and usually rise above that manufactured ceiling.

The flip side of the coin is that in capitalist societies, an individual can, and usually, will fall below the acceptable standard of living, but on the other hand can rise to achieve amazing success, greatly surpassing the ceiling.

There is an old belief that no one can get super rich in his or her lifetime doing everything within the legal limits of the law. For a very long time, this association may have been true, but with today's high technology and super creative individuals, this saying has proven itself to be less true. Imagine companies, such as Google and Microsoft, that were not household names twenty years ago. Today many of the self-made millionaires and billionaires throughout the world are relatively young and are in the technology areas.

One may argue that because socialist or Marxist societies tend to provide their citizens with at least a floor or basic standard of living, citizens of such Marxist and socialist societies are somewhat handicapped within the creative arena. In short, it can be argued that governments that provide their citizens with a guaranteed minimum standard of living also serve to limit the creativity of their citizens. A trade off exists in creativity between capitalist societies and socialist or Marxist societies.

However, my contention is that both societies have their pluses and minuses. The plus factor for socialist/Marxist societies is the reduction or elimination of abject poverty. Such societies also generally have a basic educational level that most citizens would not fall below.

One such example is the island nation of Cuba, which is located in the Caribbean. Cuba currently has one of the highest literary rates in the world. Cuba also has one of the lowest infant mortality rates in the world. All forms of education are free to Cuban citizens and there are no Cuban citizens without health insurance coverage. Every Cuban has access to free medical care.

The flip side of this coin is that the island nation of Cuba does not have many millionaires or billionaires as many of its Caribbean neighbors. However, in some of the neighboring Caribbean islands, education is not a right of the people, nor is health care a basic right of their citizens.

All in all, the old biblical quotation of "through the fire, through the flood, before one gets to their wealthy place" may not be applicable to the citizenry in socialist or Marxists societies. Once again, there is a tradeoff to be made. One cannot have his cake and eat it too. It is the belief of many, including myself, that there are strong similarities between the concept of failure and the concept of disappointment. Also, both can equip one with strong learning tools and adequately prepare one for the future. However, one's failures or one's disappointments would only be helpful in future events if they persevere during periods of struggles, disappointments, and tough times.

I also believe that failure, disappointments and hard times are all necessary ingredients to create a complete and strong individual.

CHAPTER SEVEN

STAY HUNGRY AND DO NOT SETTLE

It is a common phenomenon that after major disappointments and setbacks people tend to be ready and willing to grab on to the first opportunity that comes their way. In many instances, such actions are usually a great mistake. That can and in some instances lead to great heartbreak and long-term dissatisfaction and disappointments.

Let's take the very common experience of divorce. Although I have never been divorced, and do not have first-hand experience of the psychology of divorce, as an attorney I have handled many divorce cases. One of the major mistakes people are prone to make is falling for the first person that comes along. The reason for this can stem from loneliness. It is my belief that after the end of a long marriage, people are usually lonely and do not like being by themselves. However, being with the wrong person can, and in many cases is, much worse than being single or being alone.

A big dilemma that usually arises when such actions are taken, is what will happen when the right person comes along? I am practically certain that many couples have encountered this scenario. Even worse, than being alone is marrying hastily to the wrong person, and then the right person comes along.

This could also be true with employment. Many people accept less than ideal employment for the sake of paying their bills and meeting their monthly financial obligations. This is a noble choice. However, having a job that you do not like can have negative long-term and long-lasting effects. This is a quick reminder for people that are employed outside the field of their education simply because of necessity. Within your field of study, one can attain the highest possible level of promotion. However, working outside of their desired field, promotion is usually limited, and difficult to achieve.

Imagine being a psychologist with a PhD and working in a law school. The question is worth asking in this scenario Is the psychologist professionally fulfilled working in a law school environment? If the psychologist is fulfilled and satisfied with his or her position within the law school, then my recommendation is that they remain at that position and environment unless and until there are reasonably certain that their progressional growth and fulfillment would be met in another position within their field of psychology.

Some of you may immediately ask, what if the individual is a lawyer, holding a juris doctorate (JD), and a psychologist holding a PhD in psychology. This scenario is not uncommon. It is my belief that there would be a quasi-merging of the juris doctorate and PhD.

It is also my belief that law and psychology would become the marriage of the future. A psychologist would be a good fit for the legal profession.

My prediction is that law and psychology would be the marriage of the future.

Today, psychologists are heavily involved in the jury selection process. Hence the juris doctorate and psychology PhD combination may realize quicker success than what may be accomplished by the juris doctorate or the PhD psychologist standing alone.

I could envision a future where many of the top law schools and positions within the legal profession are occupied by individuals holding the JD/PhD in psychology combination. Such positions may also include deans of law schools.

The jury selection process is one where psychology is heavily utilized. Good trial preparation may heavily rely on the use of psychology.

Clinical Psychologist Marino Perez-Alvarez, in his article entitled "Psychology as a Science of Subject and Comportment, beyond the Mind and Behavior" described psychology as "the scientific study of the human mind and its functions, especially those affecting behavior in a given context." *Integrative Psychological Behavioral Science (March 2018)*

It may not be an abstract thought to one day, not in the distant future, for psychologists to be deans of law schools.

There was a time when the merging of law and economics was seen as the marriage of the future. However, I am of the belief that psychology and law may have equaled or surpassed the duality of law and economics.

CHAPTER EIGHT

STAY HUNGRY AND DO WHAT YOU LOVE

Remaining hungry and performing the job one loves is the key to unimaginable success and unbounded happiness. It is also the key to future innovation. In short, it has all upsides or very little downside.

There is a biblical saying, that "lazy people sleep soundly, but idleness leaves them hungry." (Proverbs 19:15) Please do not get misled into thinking that because you are a hardworking and God-fearing individual that life would be easy. Remember, there is a devil, and the devil is real.

Throughout one's life there would almost always be periods of ups and downs; times of prosperity and periods of bleakness. During such periods, the key is to always keep moving forward. There should be no need for apathy, self-doubt and worst of all abandoning your journey, your goals and aspirations. During such periods, my advice to everyone is "if you want to see the rainbow, you will have to face the storm." It is also of tremendous importance to remember that delay does not mean denial. Because the achievement of one's goals is delayed, does not mean that he or she has failed. Delay, in many instances, occurs whenever an individual is not yet mentally ready to achieve the desired goal, or lacks the maturity to handle the level of responsibility that would be entrusted upon him or her.

CHAPTER NINE

THE BIGGER THE CHALLENGE, THE GREATER THE PRIZE

The general rule is that the greater the disappointment or the delay, the greater will be the future blessings and future opportunities. One important and very common reason for delay in achieving one's goals is maturity. Many people, although they may have attained the age of maturity, may lack the mental and spiritual maturity to make maximum use of the early achievements.

Many people have commented that if they had made lots of money in their youth, they would not have known what to do with it. Generally speaking, the accumulation of wealth is not solely for the pleasure and enjoyment of the individual that has amassed or accumulated that great wealth, but it is to improve the lives and well-being of mankind as a whole. In macroeconomics, this concept is utilized to illustrate that increased wealth can be used to foster the greatest yield for the greatest number of people. The word community could be given a very broad meaning, or it can be narrowly construed. In the case of the "Good Samaritan", Jesus used the word neighbor to mean everyone that is residing on the planet Earth. Other people may use the word community to mean only the people residing in their immediate surroundings.

Even the word neighbor can have a different meaning for different people. Once again, the definition of the word neighbor would depend on the mental and/or intellectual maturity of the person using it.

Disappointments and delays usually serve to broaden one's horizon of the world in which he lives. Disappointments and delays usually serve as a catalyst for achieving one's eventual and desired goal. Not only does this serve to assist one in reaching his or her set goals, but it serves as enhancement of the activities and conduct that one should be engaged in once their goal is eventually realized.

The Golden Rule of disappointment and delay is to never quit. It is my belief that a man or woman would fail when they give up on their dreams and aspirations. Once again, we must remember that "quitters never win and winners never quit."

A life without disappointments, delays and some heartbreak is not a life worth living. There is no bigger achievement to mankind than being able to overcome disappointments and delays.

It is for this reason why an individual that has never earned anything of significance, utilizing his or her hard work, and his or her own individual efforts, would fail to realize the greatest fulfillments of life. Of course, the greatest fulfillment in life is accepting Jesus, but apart from being at peace with the Heavenly Father, individual achievements and success can and do play a major role in one's level of happiness.

Social programs and government assistance are necessary and needed in society to maintain a minimum standard of living. In terms of economics, social programs are needed to ensure that there is a floor in which no member of society should be under. However, social programs should not be meant to last for one's lifetime or for generations. They should only be utilized to get members of society to the level where they are able to swim by themselves. There should come a time when the baby wheels are removed from the bicycle and the individual can ride comfortably without it. This should be the story of life.

CHAPTER TEN

BAD OR IMPROPER TIMING

Another common reason why many people experience disappointments and delays is what most people would refer to as "bad timing" or "improper timing". There is a lot of truth to the saying "timing is everything" when it comes to realization of one's goals.

There are three factors in the value of real estate: location, location and location. In mostly all other avenues of life, success would depend on timing, timing, and timing. From Ecclesiastes 3:1-8 King James Version

1. To everything there is a season, and a time to every purpose under the heaven:

2. A time to be born, and a time to die; a time to plant, and a time to pluck up that which is planted;

3. A time to kill, and a time to heal; a time to break down, and a time to build up;

4. A time to weep, and a time to laugh; a time to mourn, and a time to dance;

5. A time to cast away stones, and a time to gather stones together; a time to embrace, and a time to refrain from embracing;

6. A time to get, and a time to lose; a time to keep, and a time to cast away;

7. A time to rend, and a time to sew; a time to keep silence, and a time to speak;

8. A time to love, and a time to hate; a time of war, and a time of peace.

Hence according to Ecclesiastes 3: 1-8, proper or improper timing in and of itself could be the determinant of failure or success. Waiting for the proper season or proper time to partake in any venture can be the difference between fulfillment and good quality of life or unhappiness.

CHAPTER ELEVEN

CHARACTERISTICS FOR SUCCESS

As stated earlier, delay, disappointments and improper or bad timing do not mean defeat or failure. However, the normal tendency of most people is to slack off, or in some extreme cases lose interest during such times. Just imagine what life would be like if everyone got everything that they desire at the exact time that it is desired. The question here is should that be the case, then what would life be?

I submit to you that a life in which everyone or most people will get whatever they so desire, whenever it is so desired, would not be rewarding. And to a larger extent such a life would be without meaning, appreciation or perseverance. The need to persevere is very special. One's ability to persevere is what in many instances separates the overachievers from the underachievers.

Achieving a goal after having to persevere for a long period of time is what may cause people to appreciate their accomplishments. Delay and disappointment are two of the main factors that can eventually induce contentment, happiness and self- fulfillment.

I can recall my late father once saying to me, "Son, it is much better if someone cheats you or is unfair or unjust to you, than if you cheat them or are unfair or unjust to them. What he was in fact saying is that delay and disappointment are usually character builders. Not only does delay and disappointment build character, but they also enhance the level of happiness and contentment one enjoys after accomplishing the task or achieving the desired goal.

Remaining hungry during periods of delay and disappointment is a very important factor for attaining one's desired success. There can be a tendency or temptation during delay, disappointment and hard times for one to give up on their initial goal, or to lessen their initial aspirations.

Ultimate success in whatever endeavor one may pursue would require one to be hungry for the attainment of his or her particular goal, and to remain hungry for the attainment of that goal.

Difficult times or hard times with unexpected negative events, may have the effect of making one change their goal, and in some events seriously question if their initial goal is attainable.

The answer in most cases is, yes, it is attainable. However, if the individual somehow convinces him or herself that their initial goal is not attainable, then it would not be attained.

Here, the power of positive thinking would manifest itself. If one believes his or her goal is attainable, the that would be attained.

You are what you think. Please remember you would become tomorrow whatever you are doing today. Hence, if one is studying to become a medical doctor today, he or she would most likely, barring some unforeseen event, become a medical doctor tomorrow.

Along that line of thinking, one may say you reap exactly what you sow. Remember, tomorrow would be here whether or not you made plans for it. Hence, why not make productive plans that will maximize our tomorrows.

Please do not view this as being unrealistic. I know that tragedies and negative unexpected events are also a natural part of life under the sun. However, productive and realistic planning would help to lessen the effect of negative and unexpected events and occurrences. Even negative and unexpected occurrences can and usually have positive outcomes. Being focused and maintaining focus are significant factors in one's ability to stay hungry. My advice to young people is to please remain hungry and if you do, your goal or goals in life would be realized.

Please remember the old Biblical saying, A good righteous man may fall seven times and rise eight times, but a wicked man shall fall one time and never rise again. What man do you aspire or want to be?

CHAPTER TWELVE

DO NOT SETTLE

During periods of delay and disappointment, one important and critical thing to do is the setting of a scale of preference or a list of the most important things that must be accomplished, beginning with the principal task. One must also remember that nothing will last forever. This is true during good times and bad times.

I can vividly remember my late father saying to me, please do not forget to prepare for the rainy days because nothing would last forever. He was attempting to remind me that good times and bad times have an expiration date. I can also recall him saying to me, during my not-so-prosperous years, that one of the biggest mistakes made by many people is that they would give up on their lifelong dreams and goals during periods of lean times. He told me about his story or life experience after the death of my mother. I was two years old when my mother died. I remember him saying to me that he could have never envisioned such a great recovery after my mother's passing. According to him, he accomplished much more than he ever thought he would have at the time of her death. He became a single father, a stronger one, and the future had many uncertainties in it. My father thought that one can accomplish much more than they usually believe when they experience difficulties, despair and disappointments.

He was telling me those things as a reminder that once there is life, there is hope and it is never over until it is over. One of the greatest lessons learned from delays and disappointment is how much stronger one usually becomes after you have been through it. The old saying that whatever does not kill you makes you stronger, is great wisdom.

BITTERNESS

One of the unfortunate side effects that can arise after periods of delay and disappointment is bitterness. This is especially true in instances where the individual undergoing the delay and disappointment was wronged. This could be the case when false allegations are made against someone, and such false allegations have resulted in loss of economic opportunities, and loss of assets and revenues.

There is a saying that after such economic or moral downturns, one can either become bitter or they can become better.

My belief is that success is the greatest revenge. Success attained or achieved after periods of economic downturns has a way of building self-confidence, pride and self-esteem better than any form of award, inheritance or windfall. I can vividly recall how I felt after receiving my Black Belt in Martial Arts. There is a sort of personal confidence one has after attaining a certain mastery of the skills of self-defense.

Mastery in the skill of martial arts creates an inner level of self-confidence that cannot be noticed or identified by the people who are around you.

It also serves to reduce fear in many areas of life. For instance, if I am walking down any street, and observe suspicious activities by an individual, or individuals, my first reaction is to get into a defensive frame of mind.

Sometimes I am uncertain of whether my years of military training together with my martial arts training have created that inner confidence and peace in me, but I do know that it exists. It is a peace and confidence that can also become violent if the need arises. It is my hope that such a need would never come to fruition. Thus, it will remain forever dormant. The bottom line is that being confident in one's self-defense capabilities usually carries with it inner peace and self-restraint.

This is somewhat very similar to periods of delay, disappointment and hardship because they breed confidence, self-satisfaction and inner peace as a result. Also, of tremendous importance is that such inner peace, self-confidence, and self-assurance, in the majority of instances cannot be detected by people on the outside.

One should not settle or reduce their goals in periods of uncertainties, hard times, delays and disappointments. During difficult times one must make a list of the things they would like to accomplish and stick to it. Please do not make any significant compromise of your goals. It is normal that one's goals must be adjusted to accommodate the changing environment and one's needs. But in doing so please do not give up on your goals. Abandoning one's goals may have the same effect as abandoning one's pursuit of happiness.

Very few things are worth having when you are unhappy. Freedom is worth fighting for, and one's happiness may be seen by many as being complementary. Do not give up on your goals during periods of delay, disappointment and difficulties.

47

CHAPTER THIRTEEN

DO WHAT YOU LOVE

One of the basic principles for success in any profession or occupation is doing whatever you love. One of the biggest mistakes that can be made by any individual is picking a profession or occupation solely or primarily for financial gains or financial rewards. Financial success can be achieved in almost every profession. It is my belief that once someone is in love with whatever it is they do, the financial rewards will follow.

One of the inescapable things of life under the sun is hard or bad times. Bad times or hard times may be different for different individuals, and for people of different walks of life. For some individuals, hard or bad times may mean lack of income or loss of employment. For other individuals, hard times may mean the loss of real property or real estate. It may mean legal trouble, divorces and other circumstances such as the death of a child. It is not natural for a child to predecease his or her parents. The natural order of things is that the parents should die before their children. But this is not always the case. There is an old Caribbean saying that green mangoes sometimes will fall before the ripe ones, meaning that a child may predecease their parents.

No matter what profession that one may choose, there will be good times and bad times.

For individuals that do not love their profession, it would be very easy to quit that profession or occupation in search of another profession or occupation that appears to be greener on the outside. Hence, the old saying, "the grass is always greener on the other side."

This is also true for a profession or occupation, and it is especially true when one is in a profession or occupation which he or she does not like.

Also, the tremendous importance is that when one is in love with their profession or occupation, it is no longer seen by them as a job, but rather it is seen as a hobby. I have heard many individuals say about their profession, "I can't believe I get paid to do this job." Or another statement that is commonly made by people that are in professions that they love is, "This does not feel like work!!" and "I cannot believe that I am getting paid to do this job." All of those statements are commonly made by people that are in love with their profession or occupation.

SCIENTIFIC BREAKTHROUGHS AND ADVANCEMENTS

One of the basic rules of life is that change is inevitable. Wherever we are and whatever we do, change and improvements will occur. In the field of science, and in many other fields, change can only be realized through research and hard work. An individual that does not love his or her job would not be motivated enough to invest the time and effort it takes to bring advancement to his or her profession.

Such change may entail further education within that field. It will also require additional manpower to make the requisite breakthrough. Those needed breakthroughs are mostly usually accomplished by individuals that are in love with their profession or occupation.

AMOUNT OF ONE'S LIFE SPENT AT WORK

A recent study from Gettysburg College stated the average person will spend 90,000 hours at work over a lifetime. Andrew Naber, a graduate from Gettysburg College in 2007, majoring in psychology and Religious Studies, and working as an industrial organization psychologist and data scientist stated that one third of your life is spent at work.

Writer Anne Dillard said, "How we spend our day is, of course, how we spend our lives." According to Anne Dillard, many people spend a large portion of our days at work. In fact, the average person will spend 90,000 hours at work over a lifetime. She went on to say that your job can make a huge impact on the quality of your life.

Andrew Naber then went on to say, "One's job usually affects their general happiness and also life outcomes."

Because how we spend our days is of course how we spend our lives, it is of tremendous importance to be employed by a reputable employer. By the term reputable employer, I am alluding to an employer whose workplace is conducted with ethics and integrity. No accomplishment in life or in this world would ever be worthwhile if it was not done with proper ethics and integrity.

My advice to every individual is to pursue your love and your passion, and in doing so please do it with proper ethics and integrity. Pursuing a job with good ethics and integrity would not preclude others from still making false claims and accusations against you, but it will place you on solid grounds to dispute it. Remember, it is almost impossible to defend oneself when they are in the wrong, but no mountain is too high when you are in the right. When one is in the right, one might even consider writing a book to share his or her experience with members of the general public. Please remember that the truth is an absolute defense to charges of libel, slander and defamation of character. Hence, my advice to everyone reading this book is that you should always tell the truth. One should never be afraid to tell the truth because of the repercussions and retaliations that might follow. The truth is an absolute must.

CHAPTER FOURTEEN

TAKE NO SHORTCUTS

A detailed examination of the life of successful individuals and successful businesses would reveal certain characteristics. Those characteristics are usually honesty, reliability, hard work and consistency. There are no shortcuts or quick ways to obtain real and lasting success. There are no shortcuts to success.

Of course, one can, by luck, win a game of chance such as a lottery. Such games of chance, like the Powerball, Mega Millions and lotto do not depend on any basic formula to be successful, but usually by probabilities and luck. I heard of an eighteen-year-old male that won over three hundred million dollars playing either the Powerball or Mega Millions on the night of his graduation from high school. Those types of situations, although very rare, do occur and would keep on occurring.

A frequently asked question is, "What percentage of lottery winners eventually go bankrupt? While it isa true saying that you've got to be in it to win it, according to the National Endowment for Financial Education, a whopping 70% of lottery winners end upbroke and filing for bankruptcy.

The Certified Financial Planners Board of Standards, Inc. (CFB) says, "nearly one third of lottery winners eventually declare bankruptcy, and lottery winners are more likely to declare bankruptcy within three to five years than the average American. According to the CFB Board of Standards, this is because winners usually become reckless with their newfound wealth. In order to avoid a harsh fate, lottery winners should not make any hasty decisions. While winning the Powerball or Mega Millions may be a shortcut to gaining wealth, there are no shortcuts to keeping or maintaining one's wealth. When discussing this topic, mention must be made of some usually unforeseen activities, such as ill health or sickness, divorce, lawsuits and forms of natural disasters that can usually serve to deplete one's financial resources and can affect one's wealth for extensive periods of time. In each of the above instances, one's age at the time of occurrence of that incident would play a significant role in their financial recovery. The younger one is at the time of such occurrence, the greater is the likelihood of achieving a full recovery. This is one occasion where the saying that, "youth is wasted on the young", may be incorrect, providing that the young would act appropriately.

The expression that all work and no play makes Jack a dull boy, is true to the extent that everything must be done in moderation. Recovery from unforeseen financial difficulties and recovery from ill health may have something in common. In both instances, the younger one is at the time of the incident, the better his or her chances of making a full recovery and in some cases surpassing his or her former status prior to the incident.

THE LIFE OF ABRAHAM AND SARAH

There are no shortcuts to success, especially when shortcuts run contrary to the law or would result in unethical or immoral undertakings. One of the most famous shortcuts undertaken in history of man was demonstrated by the lives of the Biblical family of Abraham and Sarah.

The story is well known and is well documented. God promised Abraham that he would have a son. However, because of the length of time that elapsed before Sarah's conception, she consented to Abraham having a child with her maid servant Hagar. The birth of Ishmael gave rise to the three great religions in the world today, Judaism, Christianity and Islam.

After the birth of Isaac, Abraham's second son with his wife Sarah, Ishmael, and his mother were banished to the desert. According to Adam Zeidan, Ishmael continued to play a fundamental role in Islamic tradition, which holds that he settled in Mecca.

Ishmael was born and brought up in Abraham's household. Some thirteen years later, however, God promised Ishmael would raise up a great nation of his own.

The story of Abraham, Sarah, Ishmael and Isaac fits perfectly into the saying that disappointment can result in great blessings. Ishmael is commonly known as the father of Islam.

This is a story that young people should know, mainly that disappointments do not equate to failure. Disappointments are usually the start of brand-new beginnings, sometimes greater than one has ever imagined. Many a wise man has said that failure is the back door to success. It is not what happens to you that matters, rather it is the way onereacts to or handles what has happened.

Proverbs 24:16 puts things in perspective when it says, for though the righteous fall seven times, they would rise again, but the wicked stumble when calamity strikes.

The common reality of the word falling, for some individuals, rising again after a fall may take a longer period of time. However, the key ingredient for overcoming any fall is mental. Individuals are of different mental strengths; hence this can be a significant factor in how quickly one would rise aftera fall.

The idiom, that which would not make you bitter, would make you better, can be true. However, being bitter or angry is one of the essential steps to recovery. It's my belief that if an individual never goes through bitterness after a fall, his or her recovery would take a longer period of time. Bitterness is an essential step in the recovery period before accepting the reality and hence beginning the process of risingagain.

It can be somewhat similar to the phases encountered when facing death. Psychologists Heidi Braden and Melissa Hurst have explained this to us inthe Five Stages of Dying. According to psychologists, the five stages of dying are denial, anger, bargaining, depression and acceptance. These stages are not always experienced in the linear order. The stages of death were introduced by Elizabeth Kubler Ross in 1969, in her book titled, "Of Death and Dying." Kubler Ross was a Swiss American psychiatrist. Kubler Ross spent time with approximately 500 terminally ill patients, and her book is a collection of her observations and reflections. According to Elizabeth Kubler Ross, denial begins with the initial shock of the diagnosis. They often meet this news with disbelief or outright denial. Hence, anger is usually followed with denial. Some people may ask, why me? The third step is bargaining. This stage is characterized by deal making and pleas. These pleas are often made with God. The fourth stage is usually Depression and the fifth and final stage is usually acceptance.

I hope that this chapter is instrumental in teaching that it is not over until it's over. Avoid shortcuts at all costs; but even during times of unforeseen disappointments, hope is very alive. Please remember that disappointment can cause a change of plan into a more productive plan. However, the most important thing to remember is that a righteous man may fall seven times and rise eight times, but a wicked man may fall one time and never rise again.

CHAPTER FIFTEEN

RECOVERY AFTER LOSS

The key element to recovery after loss or disappointment is to not focus on your losses or disappointment. After experiencing loss or disappointment, one's focus should be on the pathway forward and there should be no looking backwards. While it is true that to obtain growth, whether financial or emotional, one must learn from his or her past mistakes. It is almost never a good idea to live in the past. The past is already gone; tomorrow and the future is what we have left. Hence, one should learn from his or her past, but never live there.

Another reason why living in the past is the pathway to destruction is because change is inevitable. Nothing would ever remain the same. Another important factor that can play a significant role in one's success and ability to recover from loss or disappointment is the speed at which an individual can adapt to change.

The road to recovery would depend largely on one's ability to turn his or her focus away from the loss or disappointment and search for new avenues forward. According to Napoleon Hill, every adversity…carries with it the seed to unequal or greater benefit. My life experience has taught me that this is true.

However, in order to realize the opportunities created by the setbacks, one must in fact believe that new and bigger opportunities are created. This is one reason why it is a very dangerous phenomenon to live in one's past. Additionally, living or focusing on one's past means that you are unable or incapable of recognizing the opportunities that lie ahead.

While it is normal to experience grief and sorrow during times of disappointment, one should make a concerted effort to limit the period of grief and sorrow to the shortest possible time. The reason is because the longer one remains in a state of grief and sorrow, the longer it takes the world to realize the opportunities that lie ahead.

The underlying fact is that grief and sorrow are only a natural part of the circle of life, which serve to strengthen us and propel us to a higher state of mind, while enhancing our fulfillment in life. It is also my belief that the sooner the individual achieves this realization, the stronger, healthier and wealthier they would eventually become. Hence, someone who has arrived at that realization in their early twenties would have a life of endless possibilities. The words, "I can't" may disappear altogether from such a person's vocabulary. Setbacks and disappointments are desirable because in the long run, the adjustments and corrections made by the individual both serve to enhance and enrich one's quality of life.

Individuals should welcome disappointments, not be afraid of them. Within the same school of thought, individuals should never be afraid of failure. Failure is usually the back door to success. It can be a catalyst that is sometimes required in one's life.

CHAPTER SIXTEEN

DISCOURAGEMENT

Much has been mentioned about setbacks and disappointments, however there is another elephant in the room. This elephant is called discouragement. For every great opportunity that presents itself, there would also be a great or greater discouragement.

The sources and reasons for some of these discouragements may be genuine and others may be disingenuous. Some of the people that may discourage you from partaking in or undertaking any particular venture, may be doing so because they may truly believe that the underlying project that is about to be embarked upon cannot be successfully undertaken. However, there is also the flip side to this coin, where discouragements and discouraging actions are undertaken because of jealousy or for other mal intentions. Discouragements can be most damaging when coming from the people that are closely associated to you. Such people can be jealous family members or members of your inner circle.

For this reason, people are strongly encouraged to maintain a small inner circle. One should maintain a small circle of trusted friends of whom you can rely upon to almost always act within your best interest. Additionally, one should not reveal his or her future plans to many people.

The two most important reasons for mentioning a small inner circle of friends or advisors are because some people may use your ideas and patent it like it is their own. Second, some people may intentionally discourage you to impede your creative and economic progress. However, for whatever the reason may be, it is best to keep a small inner circle of friends and advisors.

ENVY VERSUS JEALOUSY

Envy and jealousy have been present with mankind since creation. Envy and jealousy go back to the days of Cain and Abel.

According to Genesis 4 and Hebrews 11:4, Cain and Abel were the first and second sons of Adam and Eve. Cain was a farmer and Abel was a shepherd. One day Cain and Abel made sacrifices to the Lord to worship and thank him. Cain brought produce from his land and Abel brought the firstborn of his sheep. God accepted Abel's sacrifice because it was an offering that came from the best that Abel had to offer. Cain became angry and jealous, and lured his brother Abel into the field and killed him with a rock.

The Webster dictionary describes envy as "resentful desire for another's possession or advantages." The Webster dictionary definition of jealousy is being "fearful or wary of being replaced by a rival, or resentful or bitter in rivalry. Envy means being bitter about what someone else possesses. In the vast majority of instances, material possessions are the reason for envy.

There is an old saying that jealousy runs in the same circle, meaning that jealousy is prevalent among people in a similar profession and with a similar status in life.

At the age of nine or ten, I can vividly remember my father making two distinct statements to me. The first statement was that "no one can ever keep a good man down, because a good man will always find his way up." The second statement I remember him saying to me is "it is much better to be a poor man's darling, than to be a rich man's fool."

Today, as I reflect on life, there is truth to the above statements. However, the two words that should be used in almost every productive and desirable situation are "I can." It is also my belief that whatever the mind or brain can conceive, can be achieved. This is true in almost every situation.

CHAPTER SEVENTEEN

TRIALS AND TRIBULATIONS

The word tribulation is defined in the Webster's New College Dictionary as a great trial, affliction or distress. It is my belief that life would be meaningless if one did not experience trials. Trials and tribulations serve to increase individuals' appreciation for the things and people around them. Imagine if every day was bright and sunny, then there would be no appreciation for the sunshine. Every day would be taken for granted with no appreciation for the awesomeness of nature. Rainy days, cloudy days and snow-filled days serve to increase our appreciation for the sunny, gorgeous days.

Within the context of everyday life, tribulations serve to produce perseverance. The primary role of perseverance is to produce character, and character produces hope.

Within the Biblical community, it is usually believed that character produces hope, and hope does not disappoint.

Character is defined in the Webster's New College Dictionary as "the combination of emotional, intellectual and moral qualities distinguishing one person or group from another." Character can also be defined as a distinctive feature or attribute.

Character can be described as what someone willor will not do when no one is there to observe their actions, or what people would or would not do when no one is looking. It should be realized that anyone who has the gift of breath will encounter trials and tribulations. However, both trial and tribulation produce patience. Trials are usually of a short duration, while tribulations are usually of a long duration. Both trials and tribulations serve to produce hope and with hope one can envision a brighter future.

The result is that both trials and tribulations are difficult when one is going through them, but both serve to be beneficial after they have ended. The endproduct is that they both produce a better and well tested individual.

CHAPTER EIGHTEEN

FAILURE IS THE BACK DOOR TO SUCCESS

Failure is usually one of the most noble events experienced by an individual. It's my belief that one usually learns more from failure than from success. That is one of the primary reasons why people or an individual should experience failure at least twice in significant events before experiencing long term and stable success.

The terms "long term" and "stable success" are used, in this context, to differentiate between quick success, as opposed to long term success which can last a lifetime. Within Christian circles, it is said that the bigger the challenge, the greater will be the prize. There is also a Biblical saying that through the fire, through the flood, before one gets to their wealthy and happy place.

The common theme in these sayings is that disappointment should be expected before one's ultimate success.

This theme can be traced back to the Garden of Eden. Adam, the first man created by God turned out to be a failure, which led to the fall of mankind. Adam and Eve were removed from the Garden of Eden and placed in a location thirteen miles away from the Garden of Eden, where they survived by the sweat of their brows and by the labor of their bodies.

The story of Adam and Eve readily depicts or illustrates the fall of mankind. When God created Adam, he was not supposed to die. The death of Adam and of all mankind came about only after Adam disobeyed God. The physical death of the human body was brought about through sin, which directly resulted in the separation of man from God. Adam was told, "from the dirt you came and from the dirt you will return." This concept is known in the Christian world as a curse from God to Adam and to all mankind.

Adam and Eve were driven out of the Garden of Eden to a location thirteen miles away. That is the reason why the number Thirteen is referred to as the "unlucky Number Thirteen."

To correct Adam's misfortune, God sent his only son, Jesus Christ, to correct Adam's problem. Hence, that's the reason why Jesus Christ is referred to by many within the faith as the second Adam. Others within the faith community refer to Jesus Christ as the Great Hope. However, I refer to Jesus Christ as our only hope.

Some of other things said about failure are as follows:

(a) One learns more from his or her failure than fromone's success.

(b) Failure is more noble than success.

(c) One is not really ready for success, until and unlesshe or she experiences defeat, and

(d) You are not really somebody until and

unless youwere a nobody.

Other very important folklores are (a) Failure is the back door to success.

(b) Every successful man or woman has experienced failure at least twice in their lives before he or she has achieved success.

All of the above folklores are saying something very similar and that is, that failure in one's life is inevitable. It is never if failure would occur in one's life, but when it would eventually occur. This same sentiment is written in the Bible, when God said "he promised us life, but he never promised us a life free of troubles, heartbreak and disappointments." The manner in which one reacts to or handles failure is a strong determinant of how far up the social ladder, the economic ladder or political ladder would be achieved. There is another old saying that ten percent of one's life would be determined by the things, events and disappointments that one encounters, but ninety percent of success or failure would be determined by the manner in which one reacts or handles the pleasant and unpleasant events of his or her life.

The fall of mankind refers to the death of the human body. Man was not created to die. Upon the creation of man, it was God's hope and intention that man would live forever. Physical death was brought upon mankind because of the sin of Adam and Eve. As we all should know, all of mankind and womankind are descendants of Adam and Eve, the two first people created by God.

It is a fundamental truth that people learn more from their mistakes than from their success. Along this train of thought, it is very commonly said that losing is more noble than winning. The reality of life is that failure is the back door to success.

There is an old saying that in order for one to become a good leader, they must first learn to be a good follower. However, in an imperfect world, with the abundance of deceit and untrustworthiness that is prevalent in society, most people would opt for immediate leadership because of the gigantic level of distrust among members of society.

In conclusion, disappointments, trials, tribulations and failures usually lead to the same conclusion. That is to a divine connection and realization which can ultimately lead to a happy wonderful thereafter.

69